A Gift For: ELISE & DYLAN

From: GRANDMA PAT

Hallmark

Copyright © 2016 Hallmark Licensing, LLC

Published by Hallmark Gift Books,
a division of Hallmark Cards, Inc.,
Kansas City, MO 64141
Visit us on the Web at Hallmark.com.

All rights reserved. No part of this publication may be reproduced, transmitted, or stored in any form or by any means without the prior written permission of the publisher.

Editorial Director: Delia Berrigan
Editors: Chelsea Resnick and Kim Schworm Acosta
Art Director: Chris Opheim
Designer/Production Designer: Dan Horton

ISBN: 978-1-63059-882-2
BOK1199
Made in China

1118

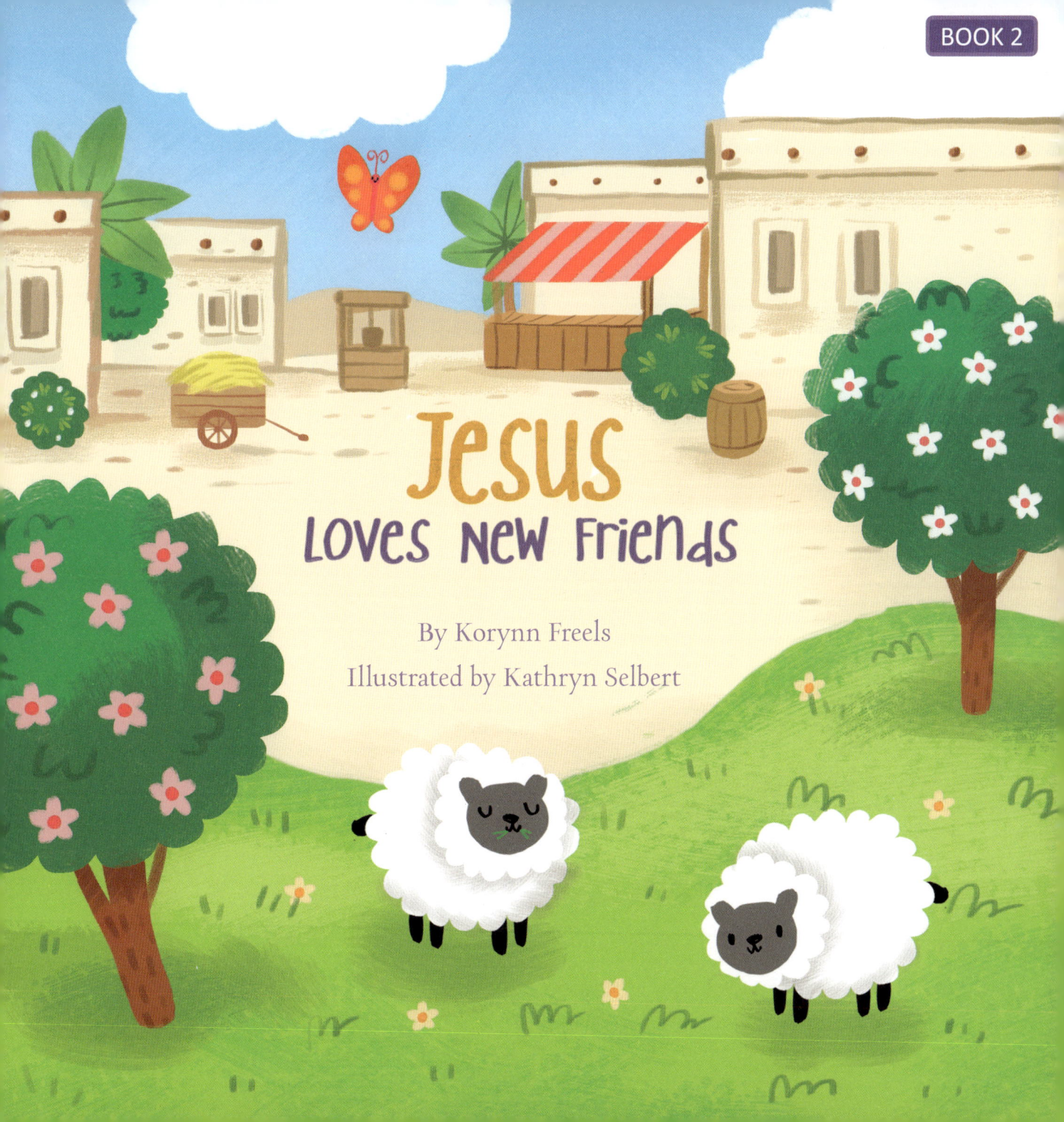

Whenever people felt alone,
Jesus went and found them.
He knew they'd make amazing friends
and loved to be around them.

A woman from another land was visiting a well. She didn't have the same beliefs, and everyone could tell.

But Jesus wanted to be friends.
He didn't walk away.
The woman was so happy
to meet Jesus on that day!

Zacchaeus had a job collecting money for the king. (Most people didn't like the ones who did this sort of thing.)

See, Jesus loves all kinds of friends together having fun.
We may not think or look alike, but in God, we are one!

Did you enjoy this book?
We'd love to hear from you!

Please write a review at Hallmark.com,
e-mail us at booknotes@hallmark.com,
or send your comments to:

Hallmark Book Feedback
P.O. Box 419034
Mail Drop 100
Kansas City, MO 64141

And when we live like Jesus,
being kind to all we know,
we'll feel God's love and make new friends
wherever we may go!

Contents

Who Was Alberto Ruz Lhuillier?   4

Digging for Treasures   6

The Temple Search   8

Digging Deeper   10

The Hidden Stairway   12

The Burial Chamber   14

The Stone Coffin   16

Jade and Jewelry   18

Mystery Behind the Mask   20

Exploring More   22

What If?   24

Index   24

Who Was Alberto Ruz Lhuillier?

Alberto Ruz Lhuillier was an archaeologist whose curiosity and passion for Maya culture led him to discover the royal tomb of Lord Pacal at Palenque (*Pah LANE kay*) in Mexico.

Alberto's family was originally from Cuba, but Alberto was born in France. When he was a young man of 22, his parents sent him back to Cuba, where he learned about his heritage. Eventually, he left Cuba and settled in Mexico. In his adopted homeland, he studied to be an archaeologist.

1906	1935	1943	1949
Alberto Ruz Lhuillier is born in France.	Alberto leaves Cuba to live and study in Mexico.	Alberto becomes an apprentice archaeologist.	Alberto is named director of research at Palenque.

Setting the Scene

The Maya City

The ancient Maya city of Palenque is located in southern Mexico, near the border of Guatemala. It is in the state of Chiapas.

The Temple of Inscriptions

This pyramid, with its five doorways, is an impressive sight. It is the tallest pyramid in the city of Palenque.

1949
In May, Alberto finds a blocked underground passageway in the Temple of Inscriptions.

1952
In July, Alberto enters the royal tomb hidden deep under the ground.

1974
The unknown ruler is identified as the great Lord Pacal.

1979
Alberto dies. He is buried near the Temple of Inscriptions.

Digging for Treasures

1943

Alberto kneeled on the ground, smiling as he worked. He was happy to be working on such an important archaeological dig. It is what he liked to do most. He was digging for treasures with one of the great archaeologists of Mexico. He tried to learn as much as he could from this great scholar.

Although he was happy, Alberto was tired. He had been working all day without a break, but he carefully kept scraping away the dirt, stone by stone. He hoped to unearth something before he stopped for the evening. Then, as he wiped his brow, Alberto's trowel clinked against something metal. At last, he had struck gold!

Alberto worked as an apprentice archaeologist at Monte Alban, Oaxaca. This is an ancient city where the famous Tomb 7 is located. Tomb 7 was first discovered in 1932 by Mexican archaeologist Dr. Alfonso Caso.

Tomb 7 held about 500 precious artifacts made from silver, turquoise, coral, jade, amber, jet, bone, and gold. These artifacts are now housed in the Regional Museum of Oaxaca.

The Temple Search

May 19, 1949

Alberto sat on the temple stairs. The morning fog was lifting, and the sun was beginning to warm the stone. He thought back to the 1800s, when early explorers documented the ruins at Palenque, a city that had remained hidden from the outside world for centuries. Then Alberto's mind wandered even further back, to A.D. 684, the time when the great Lord Chan-Bahlum I, or Snake-Jaguar, ruled the city. Suddenly, the sound of monkeys in the trees brought Alberto back to the present. Tomorrow, he would begin his research in the Temple of Inscriptions. He felt sure there were treasures still to be found.

document to record in written, photographic, or other forms

"I was convinced that many other archaeological treasures still lay hidden in the rubble of the palaces, temples, and pyramids."
—Alberto Ruz Lhuillier's firsthand account from the *Illustrated London News*

American lawyer, writer, and explorer John Lloyd Stephens and English artist Frederick Catherwood visited Palenque in 1840. Stephens later wrote two bestselling books about their travels and discoveries in Central America. Catherwood illustrated their findings. The books brought the ancient Maya civilization to the world's attention.

The Maya believed that the higher the temples, the closer they were to the heavens. Alberto chose the Temple of Inscriptions to explore because it was the tallest pyramid in Palenque.

9

Digging Deeper

May 20, 1949

Alberto was deep in thought as he stood on the great stone slab in the pyramid's central chamber. He stared at the holes around the edges of the slab and the stone plugs that sealed them. Suddenly, Alberto's curiosity was aroused. He wondered if the ancient Maya had sealed off a secret chamber. He asked his workers to lift the slab. Sure enough, they uncovered a passageway filled with stones.

Alberto and his team worked in cramped conditions, clearing large stones with ropes and pulleys. The fumes from their lamps and the dust made it difficult to work for long periods. It was dangerous work. Everyone constantly feared that the passageway might collapse at any moment.

chamber an enclosed space

Many experts had noticed the holes in the slab and the stone plugs that sealed them. However, no one had offered a reasonable explanation for their purpose. Therefore, Alberto decided to focus his research on the slab. Then he noticed that the walls of the temple continued below the floor. He concluded that there was something underneath.

Alberto had discovered an internal staircase going down into the pyramid. The builders of the staircase had intentionally blocked the entranceway with large stones.

The Hidden Stairway

July 1952

After months of clearing away stones, Alberto and his team were only 45 steps down. The staircase then reached a landing, took a U-turn, and descended 21 steps deeper into the core of the pyramid. Alberto discovered jade objects in a stone box that appeared to be offerings to the gods. At last, he was sure someone of importance was buried below.

The workers tore down a thick stone wall that blocked the way. The lime that cemented the wall together burned and cracked the workers' hands, but still they carried on. Then behind the wall, they found yet another entrance. This one was blocked by a triangular slab of stone. Alberto smiled with absolute joy when he saw the obstacle. He knew he was nearly there.

obstacle an object that gets in your way

Alberto decided to explore the underground stairway despite the hard work that it involved. It took four sessions of work just to clear the hundreds of tons of rocks. Each session lasted almost three months. The sessions were spread over a period of three years.

This model, a cross section of the Temple of Inscriptions, shows the internal staircase leading from the temple floor to the tomb chamber below. The model gives an idea of the distance Alberto and his team had to dig and clear away.

The Burial Chamber

July 15, 1952

The triangular stone door was an exciting find, but what truly delighted Alberto was finding a cist that contained the bones of six skeletons. The bones belonged to people who had been sacrificed to guard and serve the dead person's spirit in the next world. Alberto knew something exciting lay beyond the cist.

For two days, Alberto's workers struggled to move the heavy door aside. Finally, Alberto was able to squeeze sideways through the tiny gap. His flashlight lit up the dark chamber, and his eyes darted about. Nine life-sized figures stood guard on the walls. Soon Alberto's gaze came to rest upon an amazing sight—a stone coffin fit for a king!

cist   a stone burial chamber

"Out of the dim shadows emerged a vision from a fairytale ... our eyes were the first eyes that had gazed on it in more than a thousand years!"
—Alberto Ruz Lhuillier

Alberto had discovered something equally as exciting as Tutankhamen's tomb in Egypt. This Maya burial chamber, which was 29 feet long and 13 feet wide, had been untouched since the day it had been sealed.

The triangular slab was more than six feet high and extremely heavy. With a great deal of effort, the workers moved the slab aside on July 15, two days after Alberto first saw it.

The Stone Coffin

November 1952

It had been months since Alberto had last visited Palenque. The expedition funds had almost dried up, but the rains had not. The weather had caused all excavation work to stop until now. For Alberto, the magnificently carved coffin was still as breathtaking as when he had first seen it.

Alberto was growing impatient. He was desperate to see beneath the coffin's limestone lid. When a hole was drilled into it, Alberto found that the space below was hollow. Traces of red paint were also found. This overjoyed Alberto because he knew the Maya painted their corpses with red cinnabar, a bright red mineral. It was a great archaeological moment. Alberto had unearthed a hidden tomb. It would soon be time to unearth the Maya ruler's identity.

excavate   to remove from the ground by digging

The Maya believed the universe consisted of three layers. The Upperworld was the heavens, the Middleworld contained the living, and the Underworld was the realm below ground. The lid of the coffin showed the dead person falling into the jaws of the Underworld. The sun symbolized that the person would be reborn as a god.

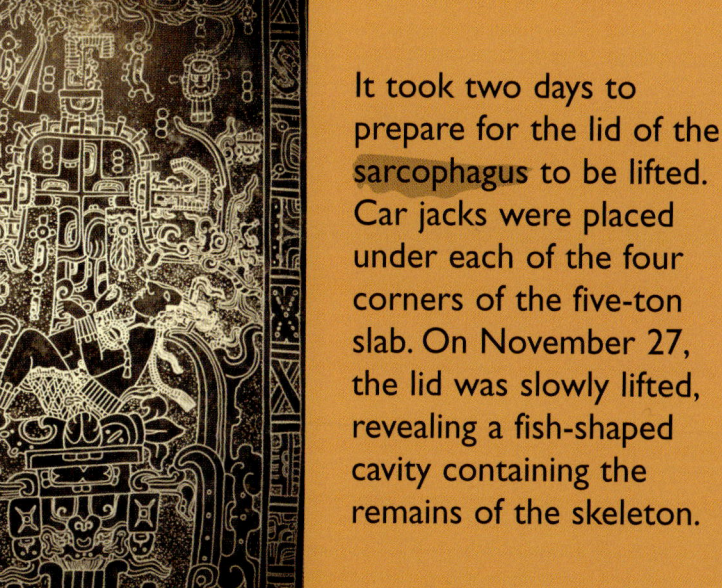

It took two days to prepare for the lid of the sarcophagus to be lifted. Car jacks were placed under each of the four corners of the five-ton slab. On November 27, the lid was slowly lifted, revealing a fish-shaped cavity containing the remains of the skeleton.

sarcophagus an ancient coffin made of stone

Jade and Jewelry

Alberto stared in wonder at the skeleton that lay in the cavity of the sarcophagus. It had been wrapped in cotton and then covered with cinnabar. In addition, the bones and teeth were painted red.

The skeleton was festooned with jade and jewelry. There was a jade ring on each finger. The right hand held a jade cube, and the left hand held a jade sphere. A jade bead had been placed in the mouth of the skeleton to ensure that the person's spirit could buy food and drink in the next world. Furthermore, scattered fragments of a jade death mask lay near the skull. Alberto was spellbound. He felt honored to be the first person in centuries to meet this high-ranking Maya ruler.

festoon to adorn or cover with decorations

> "We were struck by his stature, greater than that of the average Mayan of today."
> —Alberto Ruz Lhuillier

The skeleton was adorned with a great deal of jewelry: rings, bracelets, earplugs, a neck collar, a chestplate with jade tubes, and a headdress. The jade mosaic funeral mask once had white shell eyes with black pupils made out of volcanic rock.

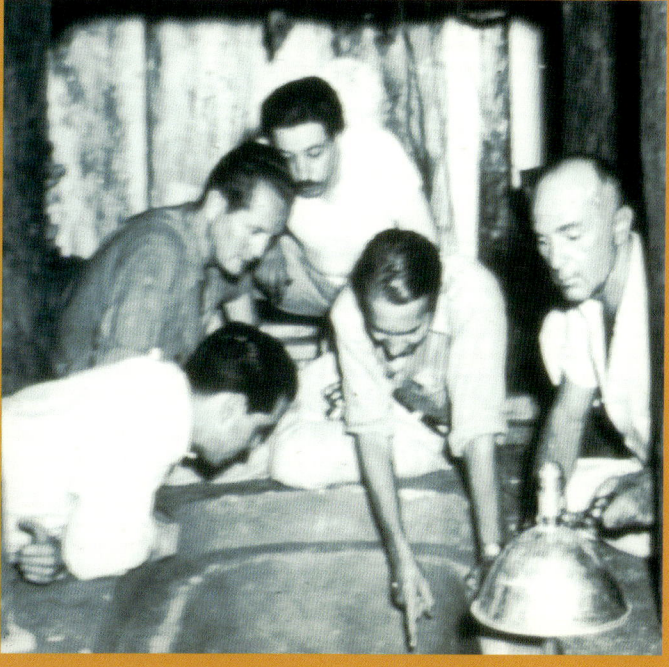

Alberto and his workers studied the remains carefully. The wooden backing of the jade funeral mask had long ago rotted away, leaving only pieces of jade beside the skull.

Mystery Behind the Mask

1974

The identity of the ruler behind the mask remained a mystery until now. Intensive detective work deciphering the glyphs, or picture-letters, on the sides of the sarcophagus revealed many clues to the ruler's identity. The mystery man was Janaab Pakal I, or Sun Shield, who ruled for 67 years from the young age of 12 until A.D. 683. He was one of the greatest Maya lords. He had the magnificent temple built during his lifetime in preparation for his departure from the Middleworld. Glyphs of Lord Pacal's ancestors were carved all around the sarcophagus.

decipher to work out the meaning of a code

Alberto believed that the bones could not belong to the great Lord Pacal, because they were thought to be the bones of a man in his forties. Pacal was supposed to have been 80 years old when he died.

Right: Pacal's funeral mask

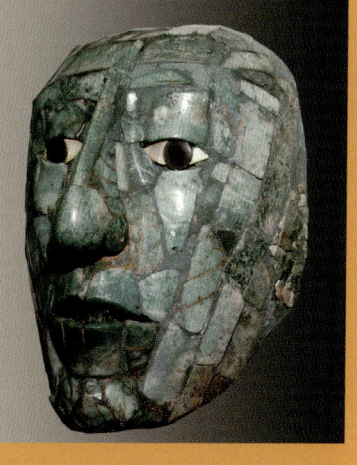

Alberto knew that he had found an important Maya person. However, it wasn't until the 1970s, when **epigraphers** deciphered the glyphs on the sarcophagus, that he learned he had found Lord Pacal.

epigrapher a person who studies ancient writings and symbols

21

Exploring More

Alberto Ruz Lhuillier contributed a great deal to the study of Maya culture by discovering the first-known royal tomb. Experts in other fields, such as the epigraphers who helped to decipher the inscriptions in the temple, also helped the world learn more about the Maya.

Today, thousands of tourists visit Palenque. However, the site is still only partly uncovered. Much of this great city is still swallowed up by the surrounding jungle. Archaeologists continue to explore, excavate, and restore the site, just as Alberto did in 1949. More recently, in 1994, the tomb of the Red Queen was discovered in Palenque. This is the first royal tomb found that was dedicated to a Maya woman. It brought newfound interest to a once-forgotten Maya city.

Curiosity and Questions

Alberto Ruz Lhuillier had the natural skills and attributes needed to be an archaeologist. He was curious, and he loved to learn about things from the past. He questioned and even doubted other people's findings. He also developed his own theories and was passionate about Maya culture.

The following are examples of other great archaeological finds.

- Pompeii was an ancient city in Italy that was buried under volcanic ash and stones during the eruption of Mount Vesuvius in A.D. 79. Excavation work has been carried out on Pompeii since the 1700s.

- In 1975, a great archaeological discovery took place near Xi'an, China. Some local farmers dug up a clay statue of a warrior. They had stumbled across the tomb of a Chinese emperor. When the site was excavated, many clay warriors and horses were unearthed.

- The *Titanic* was a large passenger ship that sank in 1912. A team of scientists discovered the wreckage of the ship in 1985.

Alberto had wanted his ashes to be buried in the jungle of Chiapas when he died. Instead, a small pyramid was built at the foot of the Temple of Inscriptions. People wanted to honor the persistent, curious man who had discovered the tomb of the great Lord Pacal, a mighty Maya king.

What If?

Many archaeologists had studied the ruins at Palenque long before Alberto Ruz Lhuillier. They had prepared detailed etchings of the glyphs that decorated the city, particularly the glyphs in the Temple of Inscriptions. However, Alberto believed that there was more to find in this great pyramid. What if he had not shown tireless curiosity and commitment to seek more knowledge? What if he had just accepted that the experts before him had uncovered all there was to find?

> **Why do you think commitment is an important trait for an archaeologist?**

Index

archaeologists	4, 6–7, 22–23
epigraphers	21–22
Pacal	4–5, 20–21, 23
Palenque	4–5, 8–23
Red Queen	22
Temple of Inscriptions	5, 8–20, 23
Tomb 7	7

commitment being involved wholeheartedly